# Fabulous
# Poems
# COMBINED

## Patsy Ruth Rambo

PROFESSIONAL PUBLISHING MEETS POWERFUL PROMOTION

A wholly owned subsidary of TBN

Fabulous Poems Combined

Trilogy Christian Publishers A Wholly Owned Subsidary of Trinity Broadcasting Network

2442 Michelle Drive Tustin, CA 92780

For information about special discounts for bulk purchases, please contact Trilogy Christian Publishing.

Trilogy Disclaimer: The views and content expressed in this book are those of the author and may not necessarily reflect the views and doctrine of Trilogy Christian Publishing or the Trinity Broadcasting Network.

Manufactured in the United States of America

10 9 8 7 6 5 4 3 2 1

Library of Congress Cataloging-in-Publication Data is available.

ISBN: 978-1-63769-616-3

E-ISBN: 978-1-63769-617-0

# Special thanks and recognition to:

- ❖ God and His Holy Spirit

- ❖ My parents (Curtis and Bertha Fulsom)

- ❖ The Oak Grove Missionary Baptist Church family

- ❖ Valliant High School

- ❖ The Southeastern District

- ❖ Dr. Darnell Wagner

- ❖ Pastor

- ❖ Librarians

- ❖ Trilogy

# Table of Contents

11

# Introduction

I was born in Hugo, Oklahoma, to Verdie Mae and Louis
Washington.
My parents are the late Bertha and Curtis Fulsom.
I am a divorced mother of three. I grew up in Valliant,
Oklahoma. I graduated high school in 1984. I attended vo-
tech school in Hugo, Oklahoma, and some college at the
E. T. Dunlap
Center through Carl Albert, Wilburton, and Southeastern,
in the study of business administration.
My hobbies are fishing and playing basketball. I enjoy
teaching children's church and doing outreach and door-to-
door ministry. I have been a member of the Oak Grove
Missionary Baptist Church in Wright City, Oklahoma since
age twelve.
I have been writing for over fifteen years. I pray that this
book will uplift and brighten your way and encourage you
in Christ and in life. May each of you be blessed by
the Author and Finisher of my faith.
Volume 1 of *40 Fabulous Poems* is also available on CD
and DVD.

# ABOUT THE AUTHOR

I was born February 5, 1966. I grew up in the country and now live in a small town. I have three grown children. I enjoy teaching children's church and the missionary ladies. I also get much pleasure in speaking in the Mighty Women of God conference. I am at my happiest when I am picking up people for church or telling someone about Jesus.

My hobbies are fishing and camping. My favorite sport is basketball. I am very shy, but a people person. However, I spend much time alone. I can listen to preaching all day. I can play country, rock and roll, reggae, and blues, but gospel is my music of choice. I like the old-school stuff.

God is good. Life is good. I plan to one day go nationwide and appear on TV. I want to thank you for your support and donations to this ministry of exhortation.

My goal is that this book will uplift you and help you along your way as you grow in the Lord. Some of the contents will make you laugh, and others will make you cry.

It is true and sincere.

Patsy Ruth Fulsom Rambo

# Poems for Christmas

# Mary, What Did You Have?

A baby boy that brings much joy. A Ruler,
an Advocate, and Bread of Life;
one who grew in wisdom and stature and never had a wife.

You had the Christ, the Mediator, a Savior for us all;
you had a great Shepherd,

a high Priest, and holy and true.

Mary, you had a Lamb, a Light, and a Morning Star;
you had a Redeemer and Protector wherever we are.

You had the Son of David, Son of God and Son of man.

Mary, you had the baby like no other woman can.

You had a Stone, a Rock, and Immanuel,

Who can go down into and come back from hell.

Mary, you had a Door, a Gate, a Prince, and a Nazarene.

You had the Word; that beats all I ever seen!

# Do You Have Room?

This thing is of the Holy Ghost
Sing glad tidings, ye heavenly host

Mary, you are about to give birth
This boy will one day rule the earth
Joseph, don't be ashamed
When she have this baby—Jesus is
His name

In Isaiah 7:14 He told you so
He was born in Bethlehem of Judea
And the wise men said, "Let us go"
They found the child, fell down, and gave Him stuff

They did not tell King Herod, because he was mean and
tough

That was Matthew, and in Luke the shepherds found the
child

He was a baby still

Simon saw Him and now could die as His will

And so, at
Twelve He knew what His mission would be
He grew in wisdom, mind, body, and maturity

There was no room for Him in the inn

Will you have room for Him, and when?

# It's That Time of Year

It's that time of year: to put up your lights

And Christmas tree
People are out shopping

What you going to get me?


You maxed out your credit card and can't get a loan

You're mailing out Christmas cards and calling on the
phone

There's no fat man in a sleigh
Won't somebody tell the story, what happened on that glo-
rious day?

It's that time of the year; it may snow and probably sleet

You cook your ham, turkey, chitterlings, and other kinds of
meat

Go visit kinfolks and exchange gifts if you want to

Just remember: if He had not been born,
He could not have died for you.

# What You Got?

Andy got a new bike to ride.

Bob got a new pickup with steps on the side.

Carol got some more shoes to wear.

Dana got extensions, a feather,

and streaks in her hair.


What you got?


Elaine got a flat screen TV set.

Fred got a basketball goal and net.


George got an iPad.

Henry got a tie, a suit, and socks to go with what he already
had.
Ida got a doll that sing.
Jack got Julia a ring.

Kathy got a fancy hat.

Rev. Lee got a lot of money, but you already knew that.

Minnie got a big box of stuff.

Nate got boxing gloves—he so tough.

Onion got a bigger shop.

Patrick and his wife got another child; they had to adopt.

Quinzella got her house bricked on half of the wall.
Raven got perfume from the mall.
Sam got another guitar to play.
And Tina got her cows plenty of hay.

Uriah got a good job that pays well.
Vince got several cards in the mail.

Wilma got lots of food to eat.
Xavier got a new stove with better heat.

Yearby got an air bed, because the one had a rip.

Zephanie got a ring in her lip.

WHAT YOU GOT?

No! No! Not for Christmas... I mean in your heart!

# Poems on the Power of God

# What's Your Story?

Paul Harvey had "The Rest of the Story" he
told

Joseph had a story; he was sold

Martin Luther King Jr. had a story—the great movement of
Civil Rights

I could tell the story of cold, lonely nights


Michael Jackson had the story of much fame

Abraham had the story of how God changed his name

Moses had the story of crossing the Red Sea

I could tell the story of what He has done for me

My parents had the story of depression, segregation, and
interrogation
down to their final years
Somebody ought to have a story from wooden floor and
pews


There ought to be a story inside you.

# Only God

Man can plant—but only God can make it grow

Critics can judge—but only God know

Astronauts may walk on the moon—only God can make it
glow


A mother gives birth—

But only God can give life on earth


A factory worker can produce products to sell—only God
can save you from a burning hell


An expert can find a diamond in the rough—only God
can handle the problem when it gets too tough

A lawyer can solve a case and you go free—

But only God can really deliver you and me

The operator can give you a number to call—but only God
could have loved us all
A well gives us water to quench our thirst—only God can
make the last be first

Teachers give lessons to educate—only God can make us
worthy to get through

the pearly gate

A chef can cook a healthy meal—only God can physically
and mentally heal

A general can lead an army of men—only God can wash
away our sin

A mechanic can take off a part—but only God can change a heart

Who has such amazing grace?

Who can enable us to cry and then wipe the tears from our face?

One day there will be another reunion in another place.

# Who's Thankful?

Moses was thankful for the crossing at the sea

Lot and his daughters were thankful God let them flee

Abraham and his son were thankful for the ram that was
caught

The multitude was thankful for the lunch the lad brought

Gideon and his army were thankful they won with just a
few

Hebrew slaves were thankful for Pharaoh letting them go,
like

Moses asked him to do

Samson was thankful for the money to pay tax in the fish
they found

The centurion was thankful for the spoken word

Eli was thankful for his voice he heard

David was thankful for God's mercy and grace

Zacchaeus was thankful for being in the right place

Balaam was thankful for the donkey being on hold

Elijah was thankful for the ax head that float

Hezekiah was thankful for fifteen more years to the good

Joshua was thankful that the sun stood

One leper was thankful, and came back and said

Mary and Martha were thankful for Lazarus, called from
the dead

Woman with the issue of blood was thankful for the virtue
that went out

Joshua was thankful for the seventh-day victory shout

Saul was thankful for the bright light on Damascus way

Woman at the well was thankful for the man she met that day

Jairus was thankful for his little girl

Sinners are thankful that Jesus died for the whole world

Disciples were thankful for the supper of wine and breaking of bread

Christians are thankful for the blood on Calvary Jesus shed.

# What Are You Waiting On?

The applicant waits to be hired on

The brokenhearted wait by the phone

The sick wait on the doctor to get there

The environmentalist is waiting on clean air

We wait for the perm to take

We wait on all the leaves to fall so we can rake

We wait on fruit to ripen before we eat

We wait by the door so we can get the first seat

At the fair, we wait in line till it's our turn to ride

We wait till the bridge is complete, so we don't fall off the side

The swimmer waits for his food to settle down

We even wait for the Little Dixie bus to take us around town

Senior citizens and retirees wait on the check in the mail

And shoppers wait on items to go on sale

Parents wait on their babies to grow

Teachers wait on students till they know

Before the farmer plants, he waits on the sign of the moon

Wives wait on their husbands to come home soon

Customers wait for the checkers to check

The concerned wait on the ambulance by the wreck

Those engaged wait on the wedding date

The cows wait on the rancher to open the gate

The enlisted wait to serve

The weight watcher waits to gain that curve

Readers wait to read a certain book

The astronomer waits with the telescope to take a look

The cook waits for the food to get done

The track star waits on his turn to run

The gambler waits for the quarters to fall

God waits for us all

**What are you waiting on...? Accept Jesus today as Lord and Savior**

# In Your Presence

I am sure Your small, still voice did call

I would have stopped to pray, but there was a sale at the mall

I enjoy being in Your Spirit and feeling You close by

I would meditate on Your Word, but I heard about the divorce and I want to find out why

If I get into the service and concentrate, I would be much better
but You see, I must finish this letter

If I lift my hands up in praise, the Spirit would flow

But it's about time for my program on TV, and I got to go

The preaching is good, I must admit

But I need to get out of here—the machine may hit

Your presence is awesome and full of power

But I am hungry; we've been here an hour

When the shekinah glory comes down, everyone will shout

I heard he was locked up—when did he get out?


If I could keep my mind stayed on Thee, and quit getting sidetracked; better get it together before

He comes back.

# What's This World Coming To?

All the talk about the Y2K computer chip.

The guys got their painted hair and pants sagging and

an earring, and they think they're hip.

Those countries continue to fight.

People walking in darkness, and Jesus is still the Light.

The bills are due and car needs work done.

People drinking and partying and think they having fun.

Hollywood will show anything on TV, and theater does

too.

Kids carrying guns to school—what are we going to do?

All the talk of sports and how many deer you kill.

Does anyone listen to the Word of God and

follow His blessed will?

Earthquakes and hurricanes do a lot of

damage to people's stuff.

You better get right before God's had enough.

Trouble in the White House, church house, and

violence and crime on the rampage.

People dying old and young of age.

Things in the sky you can't explain; yet we got

fax, cell phones, and email.

But technology or skill or education won't keep
you out of hell.
We know not the day or the hour.
Best take advantage of God's saving power.
Just look around and see in our world of today.
Christians, get up,
get busy, and let's do our job.
The world is coming to an end, looks like to me.

# What if Jesus Took a Vacation?

What if Jesus took a vacation, as we sometimes do?

In times of trouble, who would see us through?

Who would intervene for me and you?

Only God's Son would do.

If Jesus went on vacation before He was crucified,

Who for our sins would have died?

He is perfect and the best.

After listening to us, He deserves the rest.

I hope He never go nowhere.

If Jesus took a vacation, how would we fare?

He is our dearest friend.

A broken heart, He can mend.

Jesus is a Doctor and a Savior too.

If Jesus took a vacation, what would you do?

As for me, myself, I would be left, all my faults and sin to bear.

Who would take to God my prayer?

Every day my soul would say:

Jesus, please don't take a vacation TODAY!

# Poems
# About Prayer

# You Should Pray

You should pray

Jacob prayed all night

Isaac prayed for children

Hagar prayed for consolation

Habakkuk prayed for deliverance

Ezra prayed because of the sins of the people

Elijah prayed for rain

Disciples prayed for boldness

David prayed for grace

Daniel prayed for knowledge

Jehoshaphat prayed for protection

Cornelius prayed for enlightenment

The centurion prayed for his servant

Cain prayed for mercy

Asa prayed for victory

Abraham prayed for Sodom

Jabez prayed for prosperity

Jesus prayed for the church and our

Forgiveness!

# He Is... He Is!

He is my Savior—He rescued

me from sinking in sin.

He is the Door-Keeper who let

me in!

He is my Master who instructs

and controls.

He is Lord, Lover, and Ruler

of my soul!

He is my Friend who is always

near.

He is my Comforter—He calms

all of my fear!

He is my Shepherd—He keeps me

in His care.

He is my Guide who leads

me everywhere!

He is my Companion—He holds

my hand.

He is the Rock of Ages on

which I stand!

He is the Rose of Sharon—

most beautiful and sweet.

He is a Light unto my path

for my feet!

He is Christ, the Anointed One.

He is the Author and Finisher—

my faith already done!
He is a Well who freely
gives.
He is the Great Physician—
He delivers and heals!
He is the coming King—He
will rule and reign.
He is the Joy of my salvation—
He causes me to sing!
He is my Redeemer whose
blood keeps me clean.
He is my Mediator who
stands in between!

# Poems About Praise

# What Is This?

What a beautiful sound. I

hear the music all in the air…

The drumbeat in time and the

keyboard sound so fair!

Their voices are loud and

stout…

Watch the congregation when

they stand and shout!

The robes match, and the

alto, soprano, and bass arranged

as they should be…

The director out in front, so

everyone can see!

The piano is in tune…

And our spirits will be lifted

soon!

Put the tape in and sing along,

won't you…

Enjoy yourself here today—

whether many or few!

# Praise Him

Sing unto the Lord a new song, or an old one if you want to

Make a joyful noise unto God—that's what you do

Play the piano and the drum

If you don't know the words—hum

Shout and let your voice ring

Come on—move, folks, and sing

Bless His name

Declare His glory; come into His court; don't be ashamed

Fear Him; let the heavens rejoice and the earth be glad

Let the sea roar and fields be joyful and make the devil mad

Does anyone have a cornet or trumpet? Let him play

He has done marvelous things, and victory is ours today

He will judge the earth; let the people shake

Exalt the Lord and worship; come on, get awake

He answers prayer and gives success, courage, and mercy too

He has made known His salvation to me and you

Make a joyful noise unto the Lord, all ye lands

Serve the Lord with gladness; sing and clap your hands

There is hope, justice, blessings, and Holy Spirit power

Sing unto the Lord in this hour.

# Looking Back at 2006

Another year has come and gone by.

Seniors graduated from Wright City High.

Lots of wrecks and tragedies took place.

Now Obama is in the political race.

Saddam Hussein is gone, and

President Gerald Ford also.

The godfather of soul.

The ozone layer has a hole.

Talk about global warming is

heard in the news now and then.

The Razor phone is very thin.

Flava Flav is as popular as

can be.

There are iPods, DVDs, and MP3s.

Denver has lots of snowflakes.

Hawaii had a terrible

earthquake.

Fires are burning out of

control.

A woman had twins at

sixty-seven years old.

# Why Don't You Sang My Song?

There is something about the words and the sound.

I can feel something way, deep down!

I can feel warmth like oil running over my face.

Why don't you sang my song up in this place?

Start out low, then get loud if you can.

Why don't you sang my song as I lift my hand?

I can picture what you say—I can almost see.

Why don't you sang my song—sang it for me?

There is power in this Spirit, I cannot explain to you.

There is joy no matter what I'm going through.

I like that—I feel light enough to float on air.

I feel like praising Him—let them stare!

I will clap my hands and pat my feet… is that okay?

"If I Had Wings," or "I'll Fly Away."

"Jesus Keep Me Near the Cross," or "There's a Precious Fountain."

"I'm Coming Up on the Rough Side of the Mountain"!

"Will You Ride?" "Soon I Will Be Done," or "I Shall Wear a Crown."

"Glory, Glory, Hallelujah," or "When I Lay My Burdens Down."

"I Bowed Down and Cried Holy," or "What a Time," or "Back-Back Train."

"Stir Up the Gift," or "It's Going to Rain"!

"What a Friend We Have," "Amazing Grace," or "Where Could I Go?"

"This Little Light of Mine," or "All to Him I Owe"!

"Gone the Last Mile," "How I Get Over," "Nobody's Fault," or "God Is Real."

Or even "Because He Lives" or "Precious Lord"!

"Ship of Zion," "I Found the Answer," or "I Learned to Pray."

"Jesus Is the Answer for the World Today"!

Why don't you sang my song?

# Poems on Pastors

# My Pastor's Poem

He did not change water to wine at the wedding he had two
years ago.

He is not Jeremiah, but the Word is like fire shut up in his
bones, don't you know?

He is not Moses; he has walked through no sea.

But he does drive from Sherman to Wright City, and gas is
not free!

He was not on board with Noah and the rest.

But when it comes to preaching and teaching—he's one of
the best!

He is not Solomon, with riches and stuff.

But he is wise to know when something is not right—and
when enough is enough!

He is not Elijah; he does not call down fire or rain.

But he does have many demonstrations in that brain!

He is not Joshua, but he brings down the denominational
and racial wall.

He tries to unite Black, white, Indian, and all!

He is not Lot, and not the only righteous man in town.

He is not Daniel and has never been in a den of lions and
laid down!

He is not Samson; he does not have long hair.

But when a member needs him—he is strong and right
there!

He is not Gideon, with a candle and a jar.

But he does try to lead his congregation and keep us up to par!

He has not gone to Ninevah like Jonah went.

He is not David, but he seems to be a man after God's own heart.

He has not traveled to spread the gospel like Paul, but he is doing his part!

He not Belshazzar; he did not see no handwriting on the wall.

He is not Eli or any high priest, but he heard God's call!

He is not Ezra, but he explains the law and grace.

He is not Job, but he does keep the faith and waits to see what God will do.

I could use many characters, but I am through!

# Just Preach

It is worse than any cancer here.

There is only one cure, and many have no fear.

It absorbs deep within and won't cease.

The wiser we get, the more it increase.

Doctors have no medicine for this outbreak.

It hurts many people, whether asleep or awake.

This thing plagues males and females,

regardless of race.

It comes in degrees that are so high, it changes

one's face.

It destroys loved ones, schools, church houses,

and self-esteem.

It makes one act crazy and very mean.

The cure is simple—ACCEPT JESUS—let God in.

This thing is… un-repented sin.

Now the task has been dealt to your hand.

You can see the pieces; you got the plan.

Lay out what you got; they will move when it's

their turn.

They will add according to what you have, or they

will burn.

Whether you go uptown Idabel or downtown

Broken Bow.

Stay with what you know.

Keep making it plain.

There are others in this with you; some of them,

you know their name.

This isn't dominoes, or cards, or any game.

There are many in the pile you can't pull or reach.

But... yet, still preach!

# Rev. Preaches

Adam ate too much and then multiplied.

Ananias and Sapphira held back and lied.

Noah built, and then float.

When the people sinned, they had an escape goat.

Abraham had faith, and Joshua won at Jericho.

Rev. preaches hard everywhere he go!

Moses crossed and struck a rock.

Rev. preaches to the flock!

Jacob tricked Isaac and got the birthright.

Samson brought down the house with all his
might.

Daniel was in a den of lions, and Jonah finally
went.

Rev. preaches because he is sent!

Mary laughed, and Joseph was sold.

Rev. preaches, and he is bold.

Jeremiah cried, and Mary did too.

Gideon defeated with just a few!

Elijah ran from Jezebel.

Rev. preaches—the gospel keeps
one out of hell!

David was a man after God's own heart.

Rehab was a bad woman, but she did

her part.

Paul traveled a lot and wrote many a letter.

Rev. preaches to help us become better!

Peter, James, and John saw Moses

and Elijah on the mountain up

high.

Rev. preaches the birth, life, and how

Jesus had to die!

How to live, serve God, and love others;

throughout the Bible it is found.

**Rev. preaches, and so we can understand, he**

**breaks it on down!**

# Keep Doing What You Do

We see you...

We see you looking after your congregation like a nurse would do!

Comforting the hurting ones and binding emotional wounds, helping

individuals feel brand new!

We see you....

Visiting the sick in the hospital, nursing home, and at their place of stay!

On the street and in the alley—telling people "Jesus is the way"!

We see you...

Feeding chili or gumbo soup and sweet potato pie to those near!

Praying for the down-trodden and going to the troubled

homes most of us fear!

We see you...

Conducting the order of service from the pulpit!

We see you giving tapes and books to people—where they fit!

We see you...

At many services in attire and neatly dressed!

We see you wanting to be prompt, correct, precise, and nothing less!

We see you...

Concerned about the girl with low self-esteem!

And the boy who is so unruly and mean!

We see you…

Reaching out to the man addicted to alcohol!

And the woman so doped up, she is about to fall!

We see you….

Teach, tell, and advocate, regardless of what they may say!

Devote, deliver, and do work of the ministry every day!

P -Promotion

R- Restoration

E- Education

A- Admiration

C- Correction

H- Help

We see you... and GOD SEES YOU!

# Ministry and Mechanics

In the ministry—you have to get folks to start going and keep them going.

In mechanics—you do the car the same.

In the ministry—sometimes the people are moving but going wrong.

In mechanics—it's the steering messed up!

In the ministry—people may seem to be at a standstill or going backwards.

In mechanics—it's the transmission or stuck in reverse!

In the ministry—sometimes folks may go and stop and go and stop.

In mechanics—this is too much watered-down fuel!

In the ministry—when one grows weary, uplift and encourage him.

In mechanics—you would overhaul the motor or put in a new battery!

In the ministry—sometimes a person cannot see where to go.

In mechanics—you would put in new bulbs or adjust the headlights!

In the ministry—one may run ahead of God or out of His will.

In mechanics—this would be a problem with the brakes, or accelerator may be stuck!

In the ministry—someone's life may be filled with storms and tears inside.

In mechanics—you would install a new windshield and wipers!

In mechanics—when you can't fix it, you go to the manual, or salvage it.

In the ministry—when you don't know what to do, you got your Bible; you pray and give it to     God!

In mechanics—you're paid by the hour or by the job.

In the ministry—the Lord will pay whatever is right!

# Voice of the Pastor's Wife

On days like this, I get to sit here.

I am nervous, but I don't know what I fear.

I dressed best as I could.

I wanted us both to look like we should.

I have not done this until now.

All eyes on me—wow.

I am glad I got the pastor as my mate.

He is studious in the Bible and has much work on his plate!

I stand by his side and watch him lead the group.

I enjoy his teaching and preaching and when he hoops!

He's y'all pastor and mine too.

Disagree with him, but don't disrespect him; I dare you!

He gets calls on the phone night and day.

I wish y'all would learn how to pray!

Y'all invite us over for dinner or ask us out to eat.

He goes to so many churches, conventions, and congresses.

I worry about him in this heat!

I see his joy and pain.

All you do for people—you have many rewards to gain!

I wish I would have met you sooner, but the time was set.

I am the pastor's wife, and don't you forget!

I am the wind beneath his wing.

I don't do much yet but teach and sing!

I don't want to do anything to make the pastor look bad.

I think before I speak and smile even if I am mad!

I don't try to run the church, and I stay in my place, you see.

I am the pastor's wife and proud to be!

# Poems
# About
# Church

# Sunday Morning

It's Sunday morning, time to rise and get to
Sunday school so we can learn!
Get out the bathroom—it's my turn.
I got to do my hair, makeup, and brush my
teeth too.
Let's see what I wear today—so much is new!
Oh, this dress I put on is too tight.
Hurry up—you should have ironed that shirt last
night!
Do I have time for a quick bite to eat?
I found one shoe, where is the one for the other
feet?
These pantyhose are tore.
Because of the ball game last night, my leg is
still sore!
I could put the button on—where is a needle at?
Just what did I do with that fancy hat?
I'll put on some cologne, necklace, and hair
spray.
Wonder how many people will be at church today.
Got to change my purse over; have you seen
my key?

Oh my, who is that on the telephone, is it for
me?

We all in the car and it won't start.

All stations and garages are closed, and it needs
a part!

Oh, I need my Bible and book.

Here comes our kinfolks... Look!

# I Have Made Some Changes (Why Don't You)

I am not where I used to be, and I am not through.

There have been a lot of changes; let me

name a few...

There are rocks on the ground.

Inside, no wasps flying around!

The steps are low, and a sidewalk is there.

I have central heat and air!

Six restrooms, pastor's study, office, piano,

keyboard, drums, tambourine, and guitar.

In ninety-nine years, look where we are!

Cushioned pews; carpet all about.

Small windows that you can't see out!

Lights along the wall, ceiling not as tall!

Got classrooms for different ages.

Preachers who make other wages!

Don't have to bring food already

done—you can cook it here instead.

Got a baptistery; don't have to go to

Cypress or Horsehead!

A water fountain for one to drink.

Two tables: one for offering and one for
communion; even a copier with ink!
Many of the folks who used to attend
can now no longer go.
I am still the Oak Grove Missionary
Baptist Church, though!
I have made some changes; why don't you?

# Go to Church Anyhow!

I know the preacher ain't that good!

The ushers don't greet like they should!

The sermon too long, and prayer too!

The kids turn around and stare at you!

The deacons don't do like they did!

The cooks got the best food hid!

They take money for salary, robes, building funds, camps
and such!

The mission sisters laugh too loud!

The pianist sits straight and proud!

The temperature isn't right!

I was up late last night!

My pantyhose got a runner!

I got a pot on a burner!

Kinsfolks coming in!

My life is full of sin!

I need to wash, cook, and clean!

That old secretary is so mean!

I'm about to go to the show—it's a matinee!

The only time I am off work is today!

I don't think I feel well!

They scare me, talking about hell!

They point and make fun!

They hang around after service is done!

They act like big shots; they all teach school or work at the mill!

Okay, I'll go to church—I will!

At the church you will find all kinds of people, with all kinds of problems, you know!

But in order to get better, where else could we go?

But at the church there is encouragement, and they help pay a debt!

It's the best place yet!

You get revived and made to feel glad!

A shoulder to cry on when you are sad!

The Word is explained and made plain!

Some people are there to help bear your pain!

Friends on the same page assemble with those who also believe!

To worship, testify, and get relief!

Songs of Zion and full of hope!

If someone asked you to stay home on Sunday... SAY NOPE!

# Looks Like Church

I see several cars in the parking lot and smell something good to eat.

As I look around, there are folks in every seat.

The singing sounds so wonderful and nice.

The preacher is giving some very sound advice.

Folks are praying and shouting and clapping their hands.

Worshipping and praising God while they stand.

**Sounds like church!**

The atmosphere is set and Holy Spirit

moving through.

Sinners are coming to Jesus, and I am glad, aren't you?

**Sounds like church!**

Carpet on the floor, and there's a hymn.

Piano, drums, and Bibles are everywhere I look.

Cushioned pews; the benches had to go.

Offering table, communion table, and a cross by the door.

**It's got to be church!**

Indoor bathrooms, baptistery, and fellowship hall.

Sidewalk, water fountain, central heat and air, and brick wall.

Even though the building is different, the church is all right!

God is the same.

The Holy Spirit is real—let's have church in Jesus' name!

# Still Here

Church anniversary is another big day, but no dinner on the
ground is back there.

Some have fallen away, does anyone care?

Others are gone on to rest; we miss them so!

What is your purpose in life, do you know?

The dress code is new, and the building is not the original
one, as you can see.

We don't go to the creek no more when one is saved and
made free!

The wooden floor is gone, and the outhouse too.

No wasps flying around in here, and who are you?

We now have a computer, copier, and TV.

The pastor got his own office and bathroom; the deacons
count in a different room under lock and key!

A lot has changed, and pastors came and went.

Nobody pays; the church does, but more money is taken in
and more is spent!

The comfort and luxury are great, but what about being
real?

Is anyone shouting, or are they keeping still?

Are amen and hallelujah still in order, I hope to continue to
hear?

You know what else, we have Bible Study and Sunday

school classes in a different

room, my dear.

Congratulations, Oak Grove Missionary Baptist, on being
ninety-four!

Still here—and may you have many, many more!

# At the Church House

The building is brick and not wood.

In a different neighborood.

Carpet on the floor—a quieter sound.

No dinner on the ground.

A fellowship hall and a kitchen in which to cook.

A new hardback song book.

A ceiling that's not so high.

No heaters and air conditioners as days gone by.

Plants are everywhere, and light.

Christians are still striving to do what is right!

A piano, keyboard, and a drum.

Where the deacons still hum.

The pews are softer, and the chairs too.

He's brought us a long way—just look at you!

We got new faces, and may we continue to grow.

Preachers may change, but they give same gospel so we can know!

A table for the offering, and one for the bread and wine.

Looks like things are doing mighty fine!

There's a room for each class.

You can't see out the glass!

P.A. system, tapes, and baptize in any season.

An office for meetings for any reason!

Six bathrooms, and two flags on poles.

Church house is different, but Jesus still saves souls!

All the saints of old—may they rest.

Let us keep on our request!

Ninety-six years that we have been there; many years of
prayers and determination and shed tears.

Yet trying to get the salt out of the shaker.

Let us not forget to praise and thank our Maker!

# You Remember, Don't You?

Don't you remember? You should.

The old church with no cushioned pews, made of wood!

Across the road is where it stood.

The men on the left, and the women on the right.

Pull the string to turn on the light!

The bathroom was out back; watch out for the wasp and the bee.

The water was in the keg under the tree!

No classroom; each age had a place.

During service you sat still; they had a switch in case!

The brothers said amen and yelled loud.

When someone prayed, your head was bowed!

The sisters cried and threw up their hand...

Deacons rang the little bell and we all had to stand!

Church was one Sunday a month—then later went to two.

The preachers shook hands and spoke, but did not have much to say to you!

Deacons throw a hymn, then the congregation sang what they say.

Better be ready—they may call on you to pray!

Communion and sometimes the pastor's chair were covered with a white sheet.

Folks from all over town came to eat!

They cooked at home and brought it done.

No kitchen, no fellowship hall—but we had fun.

Big heaters in the winter, and fans in the summertime of the year.

No P.A. system, but you could hear!

They painted the big windows and you couldn't see the cars go by.

They stop toning the bell; do you know why?

Let us never forget the saints of old as they rest...

May we continue to grow in Christ and do our very best!

They sang with no music; had a piano, but no one to play.

After 100 years, just look at

Oak Grove TODAY!

# Is This Church?

People standing and clapping; I see them waving their hand.

Up in front of everybody, there is a man!

Nay, it's not church though—it's a rodeo.

They yelling, "He is safe!" What did he escape from?

Is he saved from hell without a doubt?

Oh! It's a baseball game; I heard them in the dugout!

I see instruments and hats on their head; there is marching and singing loud.

Oh my, it's not the choir; it's the high school band so proud.

Heads are down, and they are quiet as can be; are they praying in silence? It's a library, could have fooled me!

The food smells so good—nope, not a church—at a family reunion; have a

get-together, as they should.

I must be at church.

Not much in the offering plate; people came in late!

Babies cry and folks disagree.

Some in the hallway; others hang out under the tree!

Everyone dresses so nice; some folks don't look at each other.

But some tweak twice!

Some sit on the left, and others on the right!

Some text on their phone or listen to the iPod.

Some say amen, while others just give a nod!

Some sneak candy or a note; some are active, and others leave the meetings

and will not vote.

The pastor preaches and explains well.

The invitation is given to accept Christ and miss hell!

Love is shown and inspiration gave,

announcements given, information shared, and we are taught how to behave.

I must be in church!

We pray for one another and call;

we forgive and pick each other up when

one fall!

We are born again believers in Christ.

We are the Church.

# Poems
# About
# Growing Up

# Used to Be

Used to be green in the shed, and a green truck parked up
ahead

Used to be a goat with milk to give

A pear tree that lighting struck, and it still alive

Used to be near the hog pen was a plum tree and a peach

Used to be three pecan trees whose tops you could not
reach

Used to be a well with clean, cold water to drink right then

Used to be an old house with a potato bin

Used to be a way to hang the meat up, salt it down, and let
it cure

What is on sale?

Pick tomatoes, cucumbers, okra, and peas to sell, for sure

The figs didn't do too good, but the grapes

Blackberries and persimmons did great

Used to be corn to give to the chickens—they always ate

Used to be the mule would plow, and the tractor too

The till would make rows, but the sowing we would do

Used to be a field of corn and watermelons; they did not get
too big

Used to be a big black pot in which to cook the pig

A rub board to wash clothes

A barn and several buildings to store the feed, tackles,
tools, and water hose

Used to be a basketball goal with a net

A swing on the porch and a light

Used to be neighbors that walk you part of the way home at
night

Used to be if I had eggs, butter, or sugar, you didn't go lack

This how it used to be—DO YOU WANT TO GO BACK?

# O if There Were More Like Mine

Growing up, my parents were so strict, and

they wanted me to do right.

There was no smoking, gambling, partying, and hanging

out at EZMart all night.

O if there were more like mine!

My husband cooks, cleans, shops with me, and
calls me on break and goes to church too.

How many young Black men have time for their children?

I'm telling you.

O if there were more like mine!

My kids, as ornery as they are, they always

have a hug and kisses.

We play, sing, read, and fish; they are my buddies,

and when I'm work, it's them that I miss.

O if there were more like mine!

My friends and neighbors—we camp out,

visit, and talk on the phone about the news,

our houses; or we stay in touch and ask, "Are you doing
well?"

My church: the sisters and brothers in Christ are really
starting to grow.

They reach out to the needy, strangers, and to those they
know.

They give food, help, and pray for those who are ill.

Through the years we've had our ups and downs, but we
are trying to do

God's will!

# Poems About the Sawmill

# Now It's Quiet

Now it sure is quiet—hardly any sound.

Sadness in the air; the mill shut down.

The train still comes by, passing through.

No logs, no lumber—what we going to do?

No lines of cars going down the street.

No forklifts, no whistles, no steam from the heat.

No cinders flying, and no smoke coming out.

The office is locked, and the gates too.

There are people in there on guard—just a few.

The kilns aren't hot; there's no need.

No round out paper printed; nothing to read.

The lights are still on; I don't know why.

No sticks lay, no sawdust to blow; that was a great place to
work—I hate to see it go.

Knives don't chip and saws don't spin.

No contest, no dinners, no awards to win.

No boards to stack or bundles to band.

After it's all moved, will they rebuild on the land?

No more films to watch or records to beat.

No hard hat and no steel-toe boots on your feet.

No, the power isn't off—the economy is bad.

Weyerhaeuser Wright City closed! That sure is sad.

I could not help but cry as I thought this through.

I sure will miss everybody out there that I knew.

No gathering in the break room to chit chat.

Enjoy retirement or work elsewhere—don't just sit and get
fat.

God will help us, and I know He will.

He will see us through, even without the mill.

# Poems of
# Comfort

# I Called Your Number

I was lonely and sad.

I called your number—well, the number you had!

I knew you would not answer, but I just wanted to see.

I wanted to hear your voice and for you to talk to me!

We recalled how things used to be—Wright City is 100 this year!

Folks talked of the Hall, the picnics, and the mill,

How the stores and homes were built, and some remain still!

Churches got together—we had a good time that day.

A lot of things have changed, but we gonna trust God come what may!

We looked at old pictures and dug out old films to view.

I sure wanted to talk to you!

Anytime the church of community is mentioned, I feel proud within.

I called your number—well, the number that you had.

# See You Later, Daddy

I'll see you later, Daddy, okay?

There's a lot happened today.

It's Sunday; I went to church like you taught me to.

We had a good time, and there was quite a few.

It's Monday; I went to WMU, and we studied and ate.

See you later, Daddy;

wait at the gate.

It's Tuesday; the children went to RA/GA. I'll see you later,
Daddy.

It's Wednesday; Bible study night. We had a good lesson,
and everybody is all right.

It's Thursday; we went to revival at another town.

Hope you smile as you look down.

It's Friday; got errands to run.

See you, Daddy, when I'm done.

It's Saturday—the weekend; I enjoy it best.

See you later, Daddy... Rest!

# God Knows Best

You go on and take your rest

You grew weary, and God knows best!

Now family, don't you grieve so, and don't be too sad

She went many places and sang songs that made us glad!

She always dressed nice and looked so good

But God knows best—He is the Creator; He should!

When something needs fixing, you take it back from
whence it came

So it is with our sister; God called her name!

We must continue to live for Him, even today

He knows best and will also show the way!

The journey was long, and now it is through

Prepare and stay ready, for He will one day call you!

Cry if you must—I know you will for a while

Then think back, and look up with a smile!

If we could see the spirit realm today

"How beautiful, how marvelous!" we would say!

Tell our loved ones we will be there after a while, so we
can rest

Certainly, God does know BEST.

# Rest

Time is passing; we too must stand before God!

Let us stay working while we can!

Then, we too one day can cease

From labor here!

Cross chilly Jordan, enter His presence with no FEAR!

Sleep for a while... Take your rest!

No more of this; God knows best!

We say bye for a while!

We gotta cry, but we also smile!

In the resurrection, we will see you then!

Just rest—we miss you, my friend!

# Train Ride

Cry if you must; it's okay.

He had to catch the train; he couldn't stay.

The body was tired and he was ready to go.

He could have stayed, but God said no.

He saw the work he done and said, "That is enough, Jimmy Bee.

Come on up here with Me."

Superintendent, deacon, husband, uncle, and dad.

He just retired; don't be too sad.

Gentle-spoken, but stern when need to be.

You don't understand now, but you will see.

The glory train rides through, picking up passengers as it goes by.

One day it will stop for you and me!

# Sometimes I Cry

Sometimes I cry... Momma, Daddy, and husbands gone...
woe is me!

I smile on the outside, but on the inside you can't see.

The economy is a mess!

Sometimes I cry... I must confess!

Things happen and I don't understand; tragic disaster and
diseases—why?

I hear the news, then I cry!

We work to make money, just to spend it.

Mistreat, injustice, and misunderstood...

I know it will all end!

Stores are out of business and buildings that no longer
stand.

Technology is advanced!

Now we as a people, who did not have the opportunity,
finally have a chance.

We got a Black president in, but things were already high.

Crime is bad in McCurtain County; we don't know why...

Gambling is popular, and shacking up too.

They used to give you bubble gum and pump the gas for
you!

Drugs all over the land, corruption, and hate!

No more of this, once we get through the pearly gate!

# Attitude Toward God

# Is Your Soul Lost?

May 20, 2013

A boy lost his pet

The gambler lost the bet

The woman lost her job

The police lost control of the mob

The team lost the game

The old man lost his mind and forgot his name

My neighbor lost his key

The dog lost his owner; now he roaming free

A kid lost his gum in bed last night

The plane was lost in flight

The listener lost the station on the radio

The tourist lost the map and don't know which way to go

A teacher lost the schedule and forgot what day

A farmer lost his glasses in the hay

A swimmer lost his clothes at the lake

The model lost her hair that was fake

A shopper lost some cash

The biker lost control and had a crash

The barber lost his clippers and could cut no hair

The greyhound lost the track and left the people standing
there

The lawyer lost the case

The politician lost the race

The plant workers lost their ability to hear

Reprobate-minded folks have lost the fear

The boxer had lost several teeth out

Youngsters have lost respect, there is no doubt

Many Christians have lost their witnessing power

You make sure your soul is not lost before your final hour

# All I Want for Christmas Is for You to Be Saved

I could use a vehicle, but I got two

Admit, believe, confess, repent, and accept Jesus as Lord

and Savior—that's all you got to do

I would like the house torn down and a business in that

place

All I want for Christmas is for you to be saved and run in

the Christian race

I enjoy clothes and looking good

All I want for Christmas is for you to be saved and live

holy and not fake

I need some shoes and boots, that's true

All I want for Christmas is for you to be saved and do

what God say do

A smaller waist would be nice, and more hair

Come on up—let them stare

My motorcycle needs to be fixed, and my house painted

again

All I want for Christmas is for you to be saved and

cleansed of your sin

Lots of items in the catalog and the store

I need new windows and a door

Many women such as I would love to have a good man

All I want for Christmas is for you to be saved; is that so

hard to understand

Church could use more members, but that's not why

So you know where you going before you die

All the things I need: TV, cash, bike, jewelry, or an eight-
man tent

That's why Jesus was sent

# That's Love

He lived and went about doing good—that's good

He died—that's love

He came in human form—that's good

He came from glory; God in the flesh—that's love

He intercedes at the right hand—that's good

He walks and talks with us—that's love

He went to prepare a home for us—that's good

Where He is, we will be also—that's love

He looks beyond our faults—that's good

He sees our needs—that's love

He is soon to return—that's good

We will be caught up and changed, and meet Him in the

Air—that's love

# Where You at Now, Jesus?

You were lying in a stable on some hay

You were walking with Adam in the cool of the day

You were walking on the road to Emmaus with men who
did not

recognize You

You were in a house to escape from Herod at age two

You were on a ship, telling the wind to be still

You were getting away from kinfolks at twelve to be about
Your Father's

will

You were in the temple, driving the people out

You were in the fire with the three Hebrew boys who had
no doubt

You were at Lazarus' tomb, calling him from the dead

You were at the seashore, where 4,000 folks were fed

You were at the well, asking a woman for a drink

You were walking on the sea to catch Peter before he sink

You were in a garden, and men fell down

You entered in a locked room without making a sound

You were at the Mount of Olives, teaching the Beatitudes

You were eating with a tax collector who had been so rude

A woman touched Your hem while You were on the way to raise

Jarius's little girl

You were at Calvary on an old rugged cross, dying for the whole

wide world

You provided money in a fish's mouth so the disciples could pay

Are You in all our hearts here today?

# I Can Change Some Things

I can change my style from nappy to straight in one day

I can change where I live if I don't want to stay

If I get bored, I can change from reading this book

When I fish, I can change the bait on the hook

I change the color of my hair with dye

I can change my travel—go on a train and not fly

I can change my weight if I cut back on what I eat

I can change the shoes I wear on my feet

I can change mates when the divorce is through

If I had the money, I could change what I drive and get

one new

I can change the color of the house with paint

I could change churches, but I ain't

I can change jobs, but they hard to get

I can change hats till I find one that fit

I can change polish and earring

I can change up my voice and sing

I can change the bulb in a lamp

I can change from the lake to the creek to camp

I can change my friends and quit running with you

I can go to court and change my name if I want to

I can change the TV

But only God can get in my heart and change me

# You Ought to Move

If your house has been condemned and is falling down

If there is a snake coming toward you on the ground

If the open fire is hot and you standing close by

If a car coming your way, move—you know why

If in a meeting and asked to all sit on one side

If you at the ocean in harm's way and there comes a high

tide

If a load is stacked too high and starts to fall

If a severe storm is approaching, lie down in the hall

If that chair is especially reserved for someone other than

you

If the place where you rent is sold, what else is left to do?

If the Spirit is moving in the service and you feel good

If you want to clap, stand, and shout... you should

If the music is reaching the soul, and the preaching too

If you feel led, you ought to praise and worship God the

whole service through

# Too Late

The ballgame is over and through

The doctor is now gone; you missed the appointment

Where were you?

Class has begun; the bell rang

You missed the choir; they done sang

The sale is over; items back to regular price

The dinner is over; all food eaten but a little rice

The circus has left town

The bus has left; it is Kansas City bound

The rodeo is over; you missed the ride

Didn't get to the vet in time; your dog died

The laundry closed; can't get the clothes clean

The movie almost over; you missed the main scene

The car race is over; they closed down

The stores closed; nothing open in this town

Too late to go fishing; the sun has set

Too late to roll up the windows; inside the car is all wet

Jesus is coming back; accept Him today… don't wait

Too late

# I Feel Like Shouting

I feel like shouting… is that okay?

Never mind, get out of my way!

If you don't want to… don't hinder me

I am so happy—wouldn't you be?

I got health, strength, and I am able to go

Let me help you understand so you will know

I was adopted… that's okay!

He always blessed, provided, and made a way

I always had what I needed; He been so good

I had toys, cars, clothes, and money I did not always

handle like I should

What silver spoon you talking about?

No bare cupboard—food never ran out

Now since I been grown and run out of stuff

He always provides and sees to it I get enough

Things been tight, and I was down

No bank account, and can't get a loan nowhere in town

But when the lights off—got candles, and when the gas

Off—got electric heater and a pot

And when the money does come, it be a lot!

I have run out of fuel and not a cent to my name

But every time, somebody came

Always had a job—sometimes clients were few

No matter what—He always see me through

Parents gone, and mate too; it is sad

But when I look around, my spirit is made glad

Houses paid now, just got two, van paid and one was free

If He been good to you, shout with me

The kids will be all right

I wrote a book, and He keeps giving me things for the second
one almost every night

Not conceited or puffed up; just trying to show you how
good God is, if I can

If you not gonna shout, at least wave your hand

He protects us on the road, job, and wherever we stay

He saved us, forgives us, and we will live with Him forever
one day

Please excuse me—I feel like shouting!

# Where My Crown?

I tried to tell others about Jesus if they would hear

I knew He was returning and His coming was near

I visited the sick and helped those I could

I sinned some, but I lived pretty well

I went to church a lot

I was nice; I shared what I got

I gave strangers a ride

When someone needed comfort, I was by their side

I loved my neighbors and showed them so

When I was offered to smoke and drink—I said no!

I read the Bible many a night

Know I got rewards… that's right

Look there, how he get in?

I know him; I remember when…

A robe—what size is that?

Can I sit next to where the Lord sat?

Which mansion is for me?

Yes, stars in my crown—how many will there be?

Where is my crown?

# Who Did That?

Who put the sun there and tilt the earth just so

Who hung the moon out and made it glow

Who made the ocean and sea

Who created you and me

Who shaped the mountains and laid the desert sand

Who formed the caves, and who set the tall redwood trees

to stand

Why some parts remain dark for days

Who made the fog, frost, and haze

Why the sky above look so blue

Who makes the rain, snow, and dew

Who told the bird to fly south

Why the mother hold their young in their mouth

Where the wind come and go

Why the tide sometimes high and sometimes low

How do flowers bloom then fade

The chicken sets and eggs are laid

Grass is brown, then green

The eight wonders of the world beat all I ever seen

Dogs bark, cats purr, and lions growl

Hogs grunt, horses neigh, and wolves howl

Who does this: hurricane, tornado, and earthquake

You sleep and snore—then you awake

Babies are born

Hearts are changed and lives mended that were messed

up and torn

Who is it? You must know: God

# My God Is Real

My teeth are false; I can take them out and still eat

My nails are fake; I glued them on my hands and feet

My hair is added on—it's a track with glue

The earrings cost a dollar, and the bracelet was two

The sparkle on the dress ain't really diamond that you see

My waist is being held in; I am not skinny as I appear to

be

I am not that tall—it's the heel; the purse ain't real leather—

feel

The dress ain't gold; that's overlay

That ain't my eyebrows—that's liner drawn on; I hope it
stay

Those flowers are not blooming—they silk; that's not real

milk

That's not water running; it's an illusion trick on the eye

That's not a real bird in the cage; it's battery operated, he

can't fly

That is not real cologne, can you tell?

That's a counterfeit check that came in the mail

You can't call on that phone; it's a replica from days long

ago

But of all the things initiated—God is real… I know.

# Reasons to Praise God

He is good and has healings in His wing

He causes my heart to sing

He has given me material prosperity and delivers

me from being a slave

He is my salvation because of the blood Jesus

gave

He is my Creator and has all the glory

His marvelous works and power—what a

story

For His mercy and blessings we receive in

His name

He will rule as King and reign

# What's In Your Purse?

What you got in your pocket book?

Are there ink pens, stick pins, and safety pins—can I take a

look?

Do you have an instant camera to take a photo of where

you been?

Is there a tiny bottle of gin?

Do you have a candy bar?

Do you have an extra set of keys to your car?

Do you have the card from the motel where you sometimes

stay?

Do you have the check stub from last payday?

Do you have needle and thread, in case your clothes tear?

Do you carry a comb or brush to fix your hair?

Do you have glasses to help you see better?

Do you have that old boyfriend's letter?

Do you have money or gum to chew?

Guess you have some makeup, and perfume to spray on

you?

Hope you have your personal items; you will need those

What color is that polish for your fingers and toes?

Be sure you have your driver's license, fishing license, and

Insurance verification stuff

That purse is heavy; do you got enough?

I know you got your cell phone and pistol too

I was wondering, do you carry a small Bible with you?

Aug 2, 2012

# Attitude Toward the Pastor

# What Your Pastor Doing?

What he doing—do you know or even care?

Does he take what he makes and share?

Can you get him on the phone if you dialed and needed

to?

Is he too high and mighty for you?

Is he active in the community where you reside?

After service on Sunday, he run and hide?

Does he pay tithe and support each auxiliary group?

Does he dress decent or miss a belt loop?

Does he feed the hungry and help those in need?

Does he compliment or reward those who do a good

deed?

Does he eat all the mints and drink all the coffee because

he can?

Does he try to act like a big shot or an anointed man?

Does he shake the folks' hand and welcome all races?

Does he fellowship with other preachers and go other

places?

Does he preach the gospel and explain?

Does he encourage the members, or run them down and

complain?

Does he preach against sin?

Does he take off many Sundays and don't tell where he

been?

For Sunday school, is he always late?

Is he married but constantly trying to get a date?

Does he eat with the rest of the crew, or every month he

drives a car that's new?

Does his wife and kids look cowered-down?

Does he visit the hospital and nursing home or ever come

around?

Does he take time with kids and plan a picnic or trip?

Does he publicly smoke and dip?

Does he read his Bible and pray?

Is he really saved and walking in the narrow way?

# If You Really Love Your Pastor

If you really do… There are some things to consider; I'll name a few

When the load of church responsibility gets too much and his plate full

And things get to wearing thin

Get involved, help, and just pitch in

Let him have a Sunday free offer to wash his car or mow

Instead of him running here and there to pay the bills, tell him you will go

Offer to cook a meal or take him out to eat

Clean his office and arrange it neat

Visit those in the hospital, nursing home, and jail

Ask him: "What you need?" when he not feeling well

You don't have to wait till a special day to give a gift

If ever you see him down… give an encouraging lift

Offer to ride with or take him to his doctor visit when you can

When he is working on project, get on his side and take a

stand

If you really love your pastor, occasionally gather around

him and pray

Call and just check on him sometime during the day

If ever he does something you don't agree, talk face to

face

Don't run all over the county and throw his name all over

the place

Be in Sunday school and church regularly and bring one

or two

Be sure to pay tithe and give as God prospers you

Work diligently in the position he assign

Don't stir up problems and always run to him and whine

Keep him informed as to events and meetings in the

neighborhood

If you really love your pastor, treat the wife well.

# There Is a Man...

Alcohol or drug counselor? Sort of—he helps folks get

delivered and free and saved from hell

Bail bondsman? Maybe not, but he will come see you in

jail

Cable man? No, but he knows TV

Discuss CNN news and you will see

Delivery service? No, but if you need food, he can bring

you chitlings or sweet potato pie

Electrician? Could be, he can wire a house—look at those

he built when you pass by

Florist? He grows beautiful plants inside and out

Garage? No, he doesn't have one, but cars is something

he knows a lot about

Insurance agent? No, but like a good neighbor, he there

Johnny-on-the-spot

I could go on down the alphabet, but you know the man—

Your pastor

# Who Y'all's Pastor?

Is he one who stands by your side?

Or one who, when you need him to pray… he goes out of

town and hide?

Is he so high and mighty and too proud… he can't see

you—his head is in the cloud?

Is he one of those who does not care what y'all do?

When he gets done with the sermon… he is out the back

door and through with you?

Is he the one don't care about going higher in God—just

give him a hundred-dollar bill?

Does he protect the congregation so they don't get confused?

Or does he care how y'all feel?

Is he always late for service and gets in just in time to get

up and preach awhile?

Does he just throw a bunch of verses out there and chase

rabbits and smile?

Is he one who hoops and makes the word alive and one

can understand?

When you down and out or in trouble

does he have a helping hand?

Does he ignore visitors and overlook the little kid?

Does he complement y'all and brag on what you did?

Does he hold any titles or positions in the district place?

Is he friendly and outgoing or ashamed to show his face?

Does he use his associate any at all?

Do you get nothing but voice mail every time you call?

# You Got a Lot of P's... Let's Look at Twenty

Prayer... you a praying man

Pride... takes pride in himself and in his members

Professional... wants things done right

Progress... wants us to go to the next level

Protects... shields the congregation, guards

household of faith

Punctual... at church on time

Patience... teaches until you understand

Praiser... enjoys praising and worshiping God

Proper... knows how to talk and conduct

Polite... friendly and courteous

Pity... compassion and comfort

Pioneer... dares to try something no other pastor

has done

Purpose... a method to his madness

Problem solver... resolves issues

Personality... character

Prestige... sits with high-ranking officials

People... people person—no big I and little you

Persuades... convincing; influences and sways

others to follow Christ

Promotes... helps others to become successful

Preach... preaches the gospel well, illustrates

and explains

No one can match you... you preach with

fire!

# Attitude Toward the Church

# Don't Waste

Pour milk on the cereal, please

Put it on the cracker; don't waste the cheese

A glass of tea—sweet or green

Cut the fat from the lean

A cup of water—don't spill a drop

Pick the yield of the crop

Eat all your food on your plate

Move when you know to; why wait

Cut off the stove if the food is through

Don't blow the money; give God His due

A talent or gift; use it now

Whatever you have, put it to good use somehow

# Just Stop

You been running down your local church friends when

you can

You put down the services and the preacher man

You make fun of the choir and the director's kid

You gossip about the money you say they stole and hid

You don't like the color of the pew

You talk about those you say run the church—what do

you do?

You say they read the wrong verse and teach the wrong

lesson for today

You didn't want to come; why you didn't stay

The clapping too loud and too many shout

You may be the problem—won't you leave out

# Are There Any Christians in the House?

During offering, I see you put in the dollar

When the music fast, I hear you holler

But when the music slow, you sit down

When the preacher up, you walking around

You clap when your friend up to speak

You gossip about the one who messed up cause he weak

You talk about what others wear

Folks' loved ones pass—do you care?

You getting a pretty good check and won't feed the man

Are there any Christians in the house—just wave at me if

you can

You know if you been born again and got Jesus inside

The strait way is narrow, but the road to destruction is

wide

There are many people here today, and that's great

Why you remember to bless your food after you ate?

You won't participate in no auxiliary, nor never

volunteer to teach a kid

You the light of the world, but I guess your little light is

hid

Why you on the phone talking about what wrong he done

last year?

You run new numbers off instead of drawing them near

You drove right past her—why you not let her in?

You were in the casino last night—how much you win?

Why you so sleepy, what time you go to bed?

You dispute the Sunday school teacher—have you read?

You laugh at the choir and throw candy wrapper on the

flo'

Devotion has started—why you behind the do'?

Service going on in here—why you out under the tree?

Don't take all the peppermints just cause they free

Can't you flush it when you through?

Why you tear up the Bible and fan—they didn't belong to

. you

You never turn to your neighbor and shake their hand or

come with them to the front and pray

I was just wondering, are there any Christians in the house today?

Will you help—his light bill is due

Are there any Christians in the house—please tell me there are a few

You won't talk to me until at church, why?

I had car trouble and was walking the other day, and you drove on by

This church is 101; may God rest the souls of the pioneers and our fore-parents who had to depart

Are there any Christians in the house? Look at your own heart!

# What You Doing for Your Church?

Y'all growing and reaching out?

Are you satisfied with your few and holding on to doubt?

Are you learning and studying every chance you can?

Do you just listen to the preacher man?

Do y'all give clothes to the needy or throw them in the

green box?

Do you feed others or eat it all and get big as an ox?

Do you sing praises to God or just want to look like a star?

Do you worship the Lord or just stare or go sit in your car?

Do you participate in auxiliaries or try to knock every

project?

Do you give and support or always begging the treasurer

to pay your bill?

Or do you try to sneak to the back and steal?

Do you pray for others or wait for them to mess up, then

laugh out loud?

Are you ashamed of your church or are you proud?

Do you attend Sunday school or wait till devotion over

and through?

Do you call to encourage the slothful members and sick

or be glad they not

there and hope they got the flu?

Do you invite sinners or witness to the lost or try to stay

far from them?

Do you mostly watch TV or read and study to learn more

about Him?

Do you help keep the place clean?

Or throw your cough drop wrapper on the floor and stick

the gum where it can't be seen?

Do you contribute to the kitchen or get three plates to go?

Do you volunteer to teach a class or laugh at everybody

else working so?

Do you gossip about your sisters and brothers here?

Do you clap for the choir or put your fingers in your ear?

Do you brag on your fellow man?

Do you try to tear the church down where you can?

# I Can Get In

I can't get in the store; it is closed for the day

I can't get in the game unless I pay

I can't get in the amusement park

I can't get in the library after dark

I can't get in the White House where politicians be

I can't get in the private lodge; they won't let me

I can't get in the meeting; must be a member

I can't get in the picnic area in December

I can't get in the hair shop for my hairdo

I can't get in the sports car; it only holds a few

I can't get in the theater; I don't have five

I can't get in the ER to see him revive

I can't get in the post office for my mail

I can't get in to visit him in the cell

I can't get in the restroom; it's occupied

I can't get in the class right now; I tried

I can't get in the army and fight for my nation

I can't get in the money bag without the key

I can't get in the hunting group; I can't see

I can get into heaven—Jesus made it so

You can too, if you want to go

April 15, 2012

# What Do You Do?

Adam had to till the land

Deborah led an army band

Amos tend the flock, and David did

too

Gideon threshed wheat

Mary fixed Jesus something to eat

Samuel ministered to Eli

Saul hunted for mules when they die

Elisha plowed and Nehemiah served

for a king

Now do you do anything?

Peter and Andrew were fishing, James

and John too

What is it exactly that you do?

Paul walked the road and could not

see

Matthew collected tax like the IRS

does from you and me

John had quite a vision

The prodigal son made a decision

Sara laughed, Nimrod tried

Jesus came and He died

Now what you gonna do?

April 21, 2012

# What You Go to Church For?

May 1, 2012

You go to church often; I see you there

Sometimes you have a wig, but sometimes you fix your

own hair

Do you go to see the fellows and talk?

You sure dress up; in those high heels, how do you walk?

Do you go so you can eat?

Is it because of the guitar and choir or drumbeat?

Out of habit or tradition you were taught?

So you can pass notes and not get caught?

The church bus was the only way to get out of where you

were today?

You were sick and scared of dying, or wanted to hear

what your cousin would preach and say?

Did you come seeking to live a better life?

Or did you just want to see the preacher's new wife?

You come to show off your awards you got in school or

college this year?

Did you come because you heard they were giving away

clothes here?

Got a bill you can't pay?

Rent past due and you got nowhere else to stay?

In the morning at 9:00 you going under the knife and

may not wake?

Pressures of the world on your shoulders and you took all

you can take?

Is it because the picnic soon or the church trip and you

want to go?

To laugh and make fun of those you don't know?

Did you go to worship and praise and learn the Word?

Or you come to see for yourself what you had heard?

Did you come cause you were traveling and took the

wrong route?

All these reasons are okay, but if you come to do evil… get

out!

# Another Program

I went to morning service; it was good—the choir sung low

I'll change clothes and get ready to go

Why they always at three?

Who preaching today? Hope he not boring—I

may not stay

Are they serving food—surely they got enough

Hope they serve brisket and not chicken or

roast—last year it was too tough

Heard they got some new members to join—are

they real?

Why they build that church on top of the hill?

Wonder where the money go—their pastor

got a new truck; it's red

How come Sis. Betty Lou Marie May is the

emcee? She look so dead

How many choirs they got?

Who bought that

piano—it's too wide

Why all the deacons on that side?

Look like he got tobacco in his jaw

That's too low-cut—did you see what I saw?

The fan blowing too strong on my weave

That dummy got on long sleeve

It is five till time—where the preacher at?

I wish she would take off that hat

Wow! That bus is big—do they need all that

room?

Who is that wearing that expensive perfume?

When I came through the door the usher put a

program in my hand

Now here she come, trying to hand me another

program

June 13, 2012

# Don't Split

It happens, and it is sad

Congregations have misunderstandings and get mad

They divide and go a different way

Some members quit and others stay

Seems like you could disagree and yet remain

This ordeal causes the pastor much pain

Could they have met and talked it out—maybe so

A split

causes families to have to part

The kids are confused and lose heart

Is it really important, the color of the carpet or pew?

Being in a position with a title is okay, but you can do

what you do

Work together for a common goal to reach

Instead of him refereeing, let the pastor preach

Settle your differences before service so you can

worship in spirit and be true

Settle it, iron it out, and start anew

Don't split

June 15, 2012

# Church Running Smooth

This church is running smooth; all is great and well

We growing in number and knowledge, can't you tell?

The building is nice outside and in

We getting along and you act like you my friend

We working together to give a helping hand to those

who are new

As long as we stick together, no telling what we will do

Sunday school has more and Bible study has a bunch

More folks helping in the kitchen and bringing more

food for lunch

Visitors keep coming, and I like that a lot

Things getting done that were not

Lots of kids—we may need more rooms in the back

before you know

More people joining the choir and more giving, in spite

of income low

The outreach ministry is exciting, and inmate ministry

is helping men to see

There is salvation and deliverance, and the way you are

you don't have to be

God is real and powerful and means what His Word say

If you are lost, give your heart to Jesus, your hand to

the preacher, and join the the Grove today

Yea, the church is running smooth; may have minor

problems, but they are few

The Lord is blessing us and He ain't through

Folks taking communion and not walking out

Folks getting baptized in the name of the Father, the Son,

and the Holy Ghost

Conventions, conferences, and workshops are nice, but

souls saved from hell is what we like most!

The pastor preaches and teaches and does explain

If you don't know your job title, he will train

We have a male group with keyboard and guitar

Everyone is somebody, no matter who you are

Stand to your feet and praise His name

Church running smooth... I'm glad you came

June 14, 2012

# A Look at the Local Church

You sure are growing; you gotten big.

Nice body, laying all that weight aside

You grew up tall. I can see you blocks away

You matured in wisdom too; you seem to know

a lot

What size shoes you wear now? I see how you

walk

Your eyes are so clear and bright. I see you

Your nose developing right—it stays out of folks'

business

Your teeth are straight; I see you smile often,

not chewing up fellow man

You got strong hands; I see you hold others up

Your legs in good shape; I see you running for

the Lord

Your heart in good condition; I see all that love

in there

June 15, 2012

# Church Is All I Know

I sat in church—quiet and still

I stood in church—respect; He is real

I spoke in church—had something to say

I worked in church—nearly every Sunday

I sang in church—not a note or tune

I prayed in church—you better, He be back

soon

I taught in church—I love His Word

I worshipped in church—unique experience I

ever heard

I walked up front in church—a life-changing

event

I listened in church—the preacher

was sent

I bowed in church—I wanted to be

humble

I stay in church—even when I

stumble

I love the church—I always go

I learned in church—that's all I know

Sept 4, 2012

# Attitude Toward One Another

# In the Closet

Don't look in the closet, dear

Although it may be true what you hear

Oh, now I don't do the things I used to do

Don't be looking funny—you got skeletons too

Just let those dry bones be

Don't go digging the past up on me

It did not seem too bad back then

But the stronger we grow in Christ, the more we can see

sin

Thank God for His mercy and grace

With a changed heart and new life, we can behold Him

face to face

The blood of Jesus has washed away the guilt and stain

Don't look in the closet—what have you to gain?

Let's be the best Christians we can be

I'll pray for you, and you pray for me

Don't let the skeletons out of the closet; leave them

hanging right there

Let's press onward and don't look back in the closet, lest

it cause a snare

What you know to be bad, don't tell

What matters is that we are saved from hell

Don't make your life hard

Anyway, skeletons belong in the graveyard

# What Kind of Car You Drive?

What kind of vehicle do you drive, old or new?

Will it stop to help others and see is there anything you
could do?

Will it haul someone to your church, or is that too far?

Is it automatic or standard? Is it v6 or v8?

Will it get you to Sunday school on time, or do you be late?

Did you pay cash for it, or did you lease to own?

Will you pick up kids in it for children's church, or only
folks

who are grown?

Can Black, white, or Native American ride?

Does it have crushed velvet or leather seats inside?

How many miles per hour will it go?

How many miles can you get per gallon, do you know?

What color is that paint?

Can you let a fellow member ride, but ain't?

Can you haul some clothes or food to someone in need?

Can you take a sinner to service, or do they smell too
much like alcohol or weed?

June 14, 2012

# Where Did You Go?

I can't see you no more; I only recall

Where did you go—it was fall

I can't talk to you on the phone

This time you really are gone

We can't go eat dinner on the ground

We can't order stuff out the book

Now you can't barbeque or cook

We can't go to the lake and fish

We can't go out to eat your favorite dish

We can't dress up and go to church one more time

When I am broke, I can't ask you for a dime

We can't ride in the car and go nowhere again

We talk about the places where we been

No more killing hog, garden, picnic, or farm

No more misunderstood and no more harm

I can't see you no more; I only recall

Where did you go…I sure do miss y'all

# Do You Really Know Me?

Have you ever been in a place

And someone talks to you because they think they know your

face

They stop you on the road

Think you someone they know

They follow you in the car and flag you down

Or else they come up to you on the aisle in the store

downtown

Later they realize you not who they thought

Then they say, "Excuse me, I'm sorry" and leave the store

with what they bought

So it is with people in this worship location

We need to say the same thing and give motivation

You can't go on how they talk or smell

If they have been born again—they are saved from hell

Don't think you know them by the way they dress; their

heart could be sincere

So it is with your family and friends in here

The skirt too short, or the pants rip

You don't know what they come through—shut your lip

No particular hairstyle

Solemn look—never smile

Maybe they act what you call funny

Got a lot on their mind—the bills, the job, and the money

So they stand and clap when you don't—what that mean?

They lived a different life you ain't never seen

Do you really know them; are y'all that close and tight?

Don't treat them cold and shun them away; that ain't

right

We each have talents and gifts to use

We can all be of Christ—He don't refuse

Let's be more considerate of our family and friends—you

never know who will go far

Give time and opportunity and space—get to know each

other for who they are

No matter one's color or position in life, we are all important

to this family of God, you see

You looking at the outside, but do you really know me?

# Bullied

There once was a little freckled-nose boy

It started in Headstart; the kids took his toy

The kids were mean and he didn't understand

why

They would snatch his books and papers and

make him cry

If he was on the bus, they made sure he had no

seat

If he was eating popcorn or candy, they would

eat it or stomp it with their feet

If they had to play a game,

they would skip over him and call him a name

On the playground they were mean to him; he

tried to fight back but was not much he could do

He tried to run to the office and tell the teacher,

but she was in the lounge for lunch and not through

In school they hit him going down the hall

In the cafeteria they shoved him into the wall

They kept giving cuts so he had to wait

He was very tall

On the court they would not pass him the ball

At the track meet they would take his quilt and sack

He wanted to move, but his mom and dad would

never pack

He lived in the country and they lived downtown

If I revealed the people, you would frown

This went on from age four to the twelfth grade.

Once the boy's mother called his mother

The main problem person has changed, now is a

great Christian brother

There three or four in this group, but many others

would laugh

It was terrible for this boy... this only the half

His hair was short and grew slow

When the seniors went on their class trip, he did

not get to go

At age seventeen all this ceased, and life became as it

should be

The boy in this story was no boy at all—it

was me

April 21, 2012

# So You Eighteen?

So you think you know it all, don't you?

You still got rules to follow and obey your last

year in school; what you gonna do?

No drugs and alcohol, no talking back

You don't want to obey rules—get stuff pack

You can stay if you please; I don't care

Go to college or vo-tech or work somewhere

Still respect; don't come in all time of the night

Dress respectful, share food, and talk right

Don't be wild running in and out, or loud

No bunch over here, and don't hang out in a crowd

This too strict, get your own place as soon as you can

I am still your mother, and I'll give you a helping hand

So what if you eighteen?

# What a Mother Wants

I am a mother of three, and yes, I know

We want to see our kids doing well before we go

We try to buy what they need even if there is no dad around

We attend their school plays, ball games, and run them
across town

We don't want you to spend too many nights away

You can go on educational trips, to the zoo, museum; but
don't

forget to pray!

Church camp is okay, but be good

Eat healthy and mind the counselor as you should

In class, do your best and at least try

Think wisely for yourself; don't follow the other guy

As you get older—marry well and be true

Take care of your family and share what you do

Stay in church and raise your kids right

Pray every morning, at mealtime, and each night

Stay clean and out of jail

Work, don't party hard, leave the streets alone—we want to see

our kids doing well!

# Momma, Look...!

The house you left us burned, but it ain't fell down

There is a Black policeman in this town

I pick up more folk for church when they call

The oldest is in Arkansas, the girl got her CNA, and the

other boy sure is tall

They just won't do right—I am divorced again

I be glad when July get here! I wrote a book; it will be

out then

The mill is shut down—what a horrible sight

There are more people coming to our church, and several

are white

We don't go to Paris much no more, gas is real high

The roses are beautiful; they didn't die

There are small computers you hold in your hand

I am still trying to learn all in the Bible I can

Pastor still here, and preaching and teaching so well

We still sang hymns and tap the little bell

They play guitar, keyboard, and there are two with tambourines—

can you see?

I miss you going fishing, shopping, and to the fair with me

We have a Black president in the USA

I still remember what you taught me long ago, even today

# I Don't See Nothing Wrong

I don't see nothing wrong with what the secretaries do

They do all right, they read the reports all the way through

I don't see nothing wrong with the choir—

that was a meaningful song; I can relate

I don't see nothing wrong with the program…
they had to change the date

I don't see nothing wrong with the deacons—they look
okay to me;

those rumors may not be true

I don't see nothing wrong with baptizing her… look at you

I don't see nothing wrong with the ushers or the way they
stand

I don't see nothing wrong with that man coming to
church—it's been twelve

years; I was glad to see Dan

I don't see nothing wrong with his shirt… didn't know it
had a rip

I don't see nothing wrong with her—didn't notice the ring
in her lip

I don't see nothing wrong with the WMU; they got ten

He a member; why would he not take communion—we all
sin

I don't see nothing wrong with giving in the offering that
plants a seed

I don't see nothing wrong with letting the children read

I don't see nothing wrong with preacher's sermon… let him
stay

I don't see nothing wrong with the way the church oper-
ate—do you

know a better way?

I don't see nothing wrong with turning to your neighbor;
shake his hand

and look him in the face

I don't see nothing wrong with following the
pastor to another worship place.

# Who Gave You That?
## (skit)

I like your car—who gave you that?

My mom and dad financed it

Nice house—who gave you that?

My uncle had some of his buddies build it for me

You got lots of acreage—who gave you that?

The man at the land auction let it go dirt cheap

Mighty fine horse you got—who gave you that?

The humane society gave him to me to raise

and feed; he was being neglected

What a beautiful dress—who gave you that?

The mission sister was cleaning out her closet of

things too little

Cool phone—who gave you that?

The phone company; I renewed my contract

for one year

Gorgeous pot of flowers—who gave you that?

The flower shop; going out of business and did

not want to throw it away

Matching set of dishes—who gave you that?

Neighbors moving far away and could not

pack them; gave them to me

Fine breed of dog—who gave you that?

My cousin

That's a big pool—who gave you that?

An old friend from school

Giant screen TV—where you get that?

Uncle did not like the color, gave it to me

The cake is delicious—where you get that?

From co-worker for my birthday

You have eternal life—who gave you that?

It is the gift of God through Jesus Christ

# Poems Concerning God

# Lord, Is That You?

July 14, 2008

Use me, Lord, not just in the church; I'll go.

Lord, is that you?

I know Your voice.

I'll go; do I have much of a choice?

I know it's You speaking to my heart.

I heard You from the start.

What You want me to do?

Yeah, Lord, I hear You.

Guide me and keep me safe, I ask.

I need You to help me to do this task.

# The Newspaper

February 27, 2013

I bought a hypothetical paper, and it was not too high.

I looked in the obituary and began to cry.

It was sad… He was dead.

I could not believe it as I read;

They beat Him, stabbed Him, and hammered nails all the way through.

Why did they do that? What did He do?

He was a teacher, a carpenter, and a doctor. He wore many a hat.

But now dead! I don't believe that.

He loved all people to the uttermost.

When He left, then came the Holy Ghost.

But before that, three days later He rose.

He went to prepare us a place; He's coming back, but only

God knows.

I bought the paper, and Jesus had an article on every page.

On page one there was a fight, and He won.
On page two, sentenced to die; page three, He had a team—
Father, Son, and Holy Ghost; and on page four, ad said:
"Christians wanted, any age."

On page five was the fishing report, and it was good, but
the water sure is cold.

And you could write a letter to the editor, no matter how
old.

# That Looks So Good

February 2, 2014

The table full of food—there is meat loaf, corn on the cob,
and candied yam.

Surely I am going to eat; yes, I am.

Money coming in a few days; I'll have several twenties,
some fifties, and a hundred-dollar bill.

Surely I will spend it; you bet I will.

The festivals will be here before long—the fair and the
rodeo too.

Surely I will attend; will you?

The eastern sky will split; there will be a loud sound.

The dead in Christ will rise, and those who remain alive
will go and not be found.

Surely I will be leaving at that hour, and heaven will look
so good!

# It's In the Stars, Y'all

March 8, 2008

The Virgo—a virgin will conceive

The Libra—the price for sin was paid by the redeemer, but
you must believe

The Scorpion—sin brings death, but Jesus has the victory;
He bruised his head

The Sagittarius—the archer, Jesus, conqueror. In the lake of
fire, Satan will have his stead

The Capricorn—we needed a scapegoat; the earth was bad
as could be

The Aquarius—Living Water, the Holy Spirit, poured out
for you and me

The Pisces—the two fish, same promises in Christ, same
for Gentile and Jew

The Aries—the ram or Lamb of God, slaughtered to deliver
even you

The Taurus—the bull, judge and rule

The Gemini—God and man; ain't that cool?

The Cancer—the crab, He holds and binds us, our hiding place

The Leo—the lion, the king, worthy to break the seals; bow before His face

I found this most interesting as I took a deeper look

The stars in the sky tell the gospel story that's in the Book

The heavens declare the glory of God. The skies proclaim the work of His hand.

And by the way, Oak Grove... happy birthday and congratulations, and continue to stand.

# The Blood Still Works

April 20, 2014

My dad's old watch won't keep time—it's the hand; Mom's old cake mixer won't stir.

My Savior's blood still washes clean when sin occur.

The brakes on the old bike don't stop the tire.

The Lord's grace and mercy still keep us from the awful fire.

The old lamp won't give no light.

The neighbor's old dog has no bite.

The old car went across the scale.

But Jesus is the way to escape hell.

The old TV won't show.

What come of the old sewing machine? I don't know.

The old wagon got rusted and bent.

The old house is gone that was for rent.

The old magazine is torn and no good.

The old radio won't pick up stations like it once could.

The old can opener is dull as can be.

The old boat rotted that was by the pear tree.

But the Old Rugged Cross is still the symbol of suffering and shame.

It is where He bore our sins; that's the reason He came.

The blood He shed on the Old Rugged Cross still works. He is risen!

You make the decision.

# Jehoshaphat

2014

Listen to what Jahaziel said the Lord said for them to do.

Don't be afraid; the battle not yours, but it's Mine. March down there tomorrow and stand still and do not fight.

They worshiped God, and so did the Levite.

Jehoshaphat got a male choir to march ahead.

God caused the Ammonite and Moabite to fight the Seir, then each other until they were all dead.

None alive; all dead on the ground.

So they gathered all the equipment, clothes, and jewels they found.

They met in the valley called Berrach to this day.

They went to Judah with harp, lyre, and trumpet to praise God as they play.

Word got around their God was best.

Do what you can, and He will do the rest.

# Might As Well

May 1, 2014

Might as well praise You; You are Creator and in control

You are High Priest and Savior of my soul

You are my lawyer who gets me off the hook

You are King of kings and Lord of lords; it's at the end of
the Book

You sent the Comforter to lead and guide

You always, no matter where I go, by my side

You are the Head of the church and the Groom

You paid the ultimate price for our sin, and at the cross
there is still room

I will clap my hands and stand on my feet today

Might as well praise You anyway

# So Sweet

May 2014

You speak so softly

I hear You

Your touch so gentle

I feel You

Your presence so strong

I know You

Your love so deep

I desire You

You so wonderful

I appreciate You

You so sweet

I hunger for You

You so good

I thank You

# I Tried to Fix It

August 4, 2014

The radio would not play; the TV would not show

The microwave won't heat; the bike won't go

The toast won't pop up when brown

The roof is falling down

The record won't turn

The oven won't burn

Water line busted; that ain't no fun

Riding mower won't run

The watch won't tick and tell the hour

The vacuum won't pick up—not enough power

The lamp flashes off and on

I ran over the cell phone

The heater would not start; it was cold

The piano is out of tune; it is old

The marriage went sour and now is through

I tried to fix it, but I couldn't without You

I tried to fix it

# Thank You

December 28, 2014

Thank you... I woke up this morning and was able to walk
around

Went into the other room and the kids were still breathing,
even tho' they were still lying down

They can go to school with the other race

We have someone to stay on our own place

The elder called on the phone and was okay

We have jobs and able to work every day

We have food to eat

Change of clothes and heat

For family, neighbors, and friend

You protect and guide and bring me through

Thank you for my church, even though we may be few

Thank you for ability to teach and write; the call

Thank you for electricity, running water; forgiveness, grace,
mercy, favor, salvation and all

Thank you for the raising from Mom and Dad

Thank you for all the blessings I've had

# Poems Concerning the Church

# That Ain't All!

March 10, 2013

It has been 102 years! God is good.

You go in the work centers and throughout the neighborhood.

Races and denominations have united, but we not through.

You give away clothes and feed more than one or two.

That ain't all. Where do you go from here? What is the next
phase? This is not all.

Follow His leadership and listen for the call.

Don't just have good service, but let the power of God
come in.

Not only grow in membership, but may folks become saved
from sin.

That ain't all. Powerful teaching and preaching can be
heard in this place.

Keep walking in favor, in love, and in His grace.

# Where My Daddy's Church?

June 16, 2013

Things have changed, and we are advanced in many ways

We understand scripture we did not in the old days

We got Bibles with simple print and we can look up things
quick

Not only a piano, but a keyboard, drum, tambourine, and
guitars to pick

We got white, Indian, and Mexican too

The "fellows" coming—what did they do?

Take communion—you not worthy anyway

The blood of Jesus cleans us from day to day

They new in the area; let them join and participate

Give food to those who need it to take home after we have
ate

Let's go to the altar and pray

Bring those to church who have no way

Testify—you got something to tell

Put the names on the list who not well

Kids do great in school and got a bag

Pastor preach so hard he wipes his sweat with a matching
rag

Before Sunday school we sometimes eat donuts and drink
coffee or tea

I get to read each month when they let me

You don't have to go up to join; give your heart to Jesus
and confess, without the whole church in sight

Pants, t-shirt, and tennis shoes are all right

Anyway, my daddy didn't have a church.

# You Ought to Find You a Real Good Church

March 8, 2015

Do you go to a real good church? Where the folks try to
live holy and do what's right?

They don't talk about each other when they out of each
other's sight.

You ought to find you a real good church. If they get into it,
they make up soon. Their personalities don't change with
the phase of the moon.

Disagreements may rise, but these storms quickly pass
through.

Where the folks just sincerely love you.

The place is beautiful, inside and out.

People praise God, worship, and shout.

Christ is the main topic, and God is the reason.

The gospel is proclaimed in and out of season.

The auxiliary leaders and officers are qualified and dedicat-
ed to serve.

They are led by the Holy Spirit and not trying to throw you

a curve.

They believe in the Trinity, and baptism where the whole body is under and wet. Where they help people who are not even members yet.

A light in the community that reaches beyond its wall.

Accepts Black, white, rich or poor, abused, addicts, outcasts, and all.

Don't judge you or look down.

Don't ridicule what you wear or how bad you used to run around.

Where the fellowship is as good as the food you eat.

Where they are kind to the elderly and the children they meet.

You ought to find you a real good church.

Where they respect the pastor and treat him nice, and he in turn is too.

That's what you need to do.

Join it and attend regularly, so you can be strengthened and grow.

If you can't find one, ask me; I know.

# Who Is Running Your Church?

March 13, 2016

This church is 105 this year, and I am glad to see you in the pew

I got a question for all of you

Who running your church? Is it the ushers? They stand so straight

Could it be the WMU? Nay, they may be late

Maybe it's the Brotherhood—those men are very smart

Could it be the superintendent or Sunday school board? Those people have an important part

Maybe it's the choir—they pretty loud

Is it the deacons? They walk so proud

Could it be the children's church? They so sweet

Maybe it's the kitchen staff who makes sure you eat

Is it the finance committee or clerk, or the ones who keep the church house clean?

Is it the district moderator or the congress dean?

Is it the one who gives the most?

Well, truth is—the church belongs to Christ and should be
led by the Holy Ghost

The pastor is to direct

Christ is the Head, no matter who you elect

# Church Service

August 23, 2016

I went to the church and had a good time; there were quite
a few

I was ready to worship, because that's what we Black Bap-
tists do

The guitar started up and the keyboard, and I stood and
raised my hand

Tears ran on my face, and I shook, and my mouth trembled;
don't you understand?

I listened to the words of the song and thought about how
He uses me

I am so weak and inadequate, but He sets them free

I just invite them, and Your Holy Spirit draws and convict

# Got Hurt at The Church

October 6, 2016

Got hurt at the church—there was no preaching or singing
at that hour.

No, I did not trip on the step or get a shock from the electric power.

I did not slip on the carpet or floor and fall.

No, I did not run into the brick wall.

I did not hit my teeth on the water fountain, trying to get a
drink.

Nay, I did not get burned by the pot by the sink.

No lightbulb cracked and cut a little bit.

Nobody threw a punch and hit.

No window pane broken, nor pew.

Got hurt at the church; what do you do?

The table did not flip.

No, I was not playing with the children and hurt my back or hip.

No, not my ears; the music is okay.

No, I did not get ran over in the parking lot as I was leaving for the day.

No, my weave did not hang on the pictures and flowers when I walked by.

It was the preacher who made me cry.

# What You Doing, Church?

March 11, 2017

What you doing, church?

Are you winning souls to the kingdom as God would have them be?

Are you helping people and getting the captive free?

You been here 106 years

Are you feeding the hungry and reaching out?

Are you looking at our communities and throwing up your hands and shaking your head in doubt?

Are you just meeting on Sundays as a tradition and routine?

Are you bringing the alcoholic and dope fiend?

Is your choir just singing to sound good?

Do you praise God and worship like you should?

Are you breaking the color barrier and bringing other races in?

Are you growing closer to Him and committing less sin?

Are you supportive with your time, talents, and money you got?

Are you witnessing and evangelizing, telling the lost heaven is real and hell is hot?

Don't forget the prisoners and those who are ill.

If you just sitting on your favorite pew—don't be still.

Are you holding positions and titles too?

Are you doing what you are purposed and destined to do?

# Poems Concerning Pastors

# Supposed To

April 20, 2008

Lights are supposed to burn when they are turned on

People are supposed to talk on the phone

When you see the school bus, you are supposed to stop

The rabbits are supposed to hop

The grass is supposed to grow

Teachers are supposed to know

The job is supposed to pay

The sun is supposed to shine during the day

You are supposed to pay for the gas at the mart

Christians are supposed to do their part

Sugar is supposed to be sweet

Your heart is supposed to beat

Water is supposed to be in the lake

The oven is supposed to bake

The choir is supposed to sing

The bell is supposed to ring

Race cars are supposed to speed

A pastor is supposed to lead

The congregation is supposed to take heed

The evangelist is supposed to plant the seed

The man of God is supposed to spread the Word in this day

How else are we supposed to hear and obey?

# Don't Fall for the Preacher

June 15, 2013

He is so nice and bright

He has class and integrity and seems to be all right

His is the age of maturity and very wise

He has a nice house and car and is friendlier than most
other guys

He seems to have it all together and no points missing in
his swag

He got his Bible, notes, and materials in his bag

He eats at the finer places and stays in the five-star hotels
when out of town

He preaches and sings so well; his voice has a terrific sound

He helps you and instructs you in life

Don't fall for the preacher, he not Jesus—just ask his wife

Focus on the Lord and serve.

All honor and glory He deserve.

Read His Word for yourself and pray.

Don't fall for the preacher, cause he might mess up one day.

He only human—a mere man.

Anointed and saved as he may be, don't fall for the preacher, but for Christ only stand.

# More Than a Preacher

August 5, 2014

I wrote this just for you; it will go in volume three

You always uplifting, you always listen to me

You understand what we feel

And relate and help us heal

When I may cry, you make me laugh again

You make me seem worthwhile in spite of my sin

Whether you lend an ear or give advice

Sometimes your words cut, then you be nice

Yes, more than a preacher—you not only teach us scripture
and what they mean

You illustrate and connect; that's pretty keen

All those degrees won't get you into heaven, but Jesus will

Your works won't burn—keep working still

You call even when you're going through

We know you're human and can't do what Jesus do

God puts people in a place for a season, and that's the scary
part

Don't ever go; you got our heart

Pastor

# Poems
# Concerning
# Children

# Teach Them While They Young

September 7, 2014

Take them to church and Sunday School, teach them how to pray.

Show them attention and listen to what they have to say.

Share your day and include them in what you do.

If you go to fish, hunt, or shop, take them with you.

Keep them encouraged and look on the bright side.

When you do things amiss—don't try to hide.

Show love and morals like don't lie or steal.

When they heartbroken and hurt, comfort and help them heal.

Explain why we shouldn't do wrong—do the right thing.

Take walks, picnics, and often sing.

Teach them to sew and cook.

Teach them to think, reason, and take a deeper look.

Teach them to not be so quick to fight and run where trouble be.

Tell them, "Live like me."

Don't be a busybody all over town; make a good name and hold on.

No drama, no threats over the phone.

Work and help your fellow man when you can.

Don't follow the crowd—take your own stand.

Teach them by example while they young; hopefully, it will take.

The boy and girl they are usually become the man or woman you make.

# Don't Forget the Church

August 4, 2013

Don't forget the church, child, as you go off to college and
get your degree

No matter where you travel or what you may see

Don't forget the church. You will meet new friends and
experience much stuff

Stay with Jesus, even when things get tough

Have a good life; always trust in God; never turn

Don't forget the church, no matter what you learn

Between the lesson and work, you better find time to pray

When you get a chance to visit, come our way

Be a success and go far; we are proud of you

Your brothers, the congregation, and the pastor and family
too

Looking back, time seems to go right on by

Thank you, God, and I try not to cry

Not long ago you were on the ball team, singing in show

choir, and a cheerleader and in the school play

Even though you have grown up, don't forget the church
after today

Don't forget the church, child

# Eighteen Years Later

September 7, 2014

You carry them in your stomach, and you worry about all
the things that could go wrong.
FEED THEM

Then you have them, and they later go to school, and you
worry about all the things that could go wrong.
NURTURE THEM

Then they graduate and leave home, and you worry about
all the things that could go wrong. PRAY FOR THEM

# Poems Concerning People

# What's Going On?

2011

What's going on—on January 17 of 2011, one of our houses
burned up that night.

Van won't start, and when it does, it won't run right.

The pipes froze and busted the other night.

The heater went out and won't light.

I can't get to work; hope the patients all right.

What's going on—nothing going right.

No hot water at all, and the clothes piled high.

No money for laundry; oh, my, my.

Lord, help me; I know not what to do.

I trust in Thee; you will see me through.

No one seems to know; are they not awoke?

Can't call them, for the phone broke!

# Somebody Ought to Pray

June 16, 2013

The economy prices keep going up

While morals keep going down

Cars keep crashing

Gossipers keep talking

Technology keep advancing

But children keep disrespecting

Criminal keep breaking the law

Underage keep being neglected

Pedophiles keep abusing

Diseases keep infecting

Disasters keep occurring

The poor keep struggling

Factories keep closing

Drugs keep spreading

Divorces keep being granted

Students keep dropping out

Our men keep getting incarcerated

Homes keep burning

Hearts keep getting broken

Kinfolks keep falling out

Neighbors keep turning their backs

Churches keep splitting

Sinners keep rejecting Christ

Somebody ought to pray

# Pain On the Inside

2013

I am so lonely, it hurts within.

I have no one to talk to—an emptiness where love had been.

I sit in my room all by myself.

The quietness in here so loud, it makes me deaf.

I would cry, but what good would it do—who would hear the sound?

The children are watching TV elsewhere, and one gone downtown.

They would not understand; no one will.

I just sit here and think—no TV, no radio—just emptiness and still.

No phone call, no one comes to see.

Just loneliness, pain, and me.

If it were an object, I would tear it apart!

But it's not tangible; it's in my heart.

No medicine—what could cure? What procedure could I take?

This loneliness makes me sick—O, how I ache!

The clothes, the jewelry, not even the stuffed animals offer any comfort at all. Is there anybody else outside this wall?

I hear no traffic go by, no dog bark.

Maybe the birds would sing by my window, but it's too dark.

I could scream or yell.

But a neighbor may call Vinita and think I am not mentally well.

If only I had a good husband—a mate.

This loneliness and pain would be gone that I so much hate.

I pray and read my Bible best I can.

It's just so hard to stay focused without a man.

I was married, but now no one to hold me tight.

Oh, I can't stand this cold, lonely night.

The pain is so great.

I will be patient; I will stay strong, and I will continue to wait.

# It's Your Choice

August 4, 2014

Hot dog or hamburger

White or wheat

Plain or sweet

Fast music or slow

Hold on or let go

Leave or stay

Tomorrow or today

Paneling or paint

Do that or ain't

Sit or stand

Ignore or lend a hand

Rise high or stay low

Yes or no

Bake or fry

Live or die

Keep it to yourself or tell

Heaven or hell

It's your choice

# My Husband Like the Ocean

August 7, 2014

He is sometimes high and sometimes low.

He comes in, then where does he go?

He can be cold and hard.

He can bring life or destroy your yard.

He can be refreshing or drown.

He can carry you or toss you around.

He is strong and tall.

He can be a lot of fun; we have a ball.

Sometimes he is dangerous and bad.

Many experiences and storms he has had.

He changes with the moon.

He will be in soon.

God is in control of them both.

# At Momma' s House

September 7, 2014

You can't smoke; if you do, it's outside.

There's chicken, fish, pork chop, and it's all fried.

Tell the truth—she be mad if you lied.

If it's hot, the fan be on; if it's cold, there will be lots of heat.

Take those muddy boots off your feet.

Shut the door, wash your hands, and pray before you eat.

Pull the chair up—don't scratch the paint.

Change the subject, don't talk about haint.

You going to Sunday school—don't think you ain't.

Plenty of food, but clean your plate.

Get in by 12:00—don't be late.

Be good in school and don't fight your playmate.

Chew your food well; make sure it's not half raw.

Don't speed; obey the law.

Say no ma'am, not nay.

No liquor, wine, or beer.

It's storming; sit down and show fear.

Get right! Jesus' coming is near!

If others act ugly, let them be.

I think you can relate—or is it just me?

Can't watch no cussing on TV.

Clean the fish that you caught.

Take care of the things you bought.

Live like the Bible say you ought.

Bring the vegetables in. Gather the eggs from the hen. Feed the dog and slop the hog in the pen.

Pick up your clothes, books, and stuff.

Save up your money till you get enough.

If you fall off the bike, get up; be tough.

Put the lid down and flush the pot.

Make something of yourself—be a big shot.

I love you a lot.

# Where Your Big Feet Going?

September 26, 2014

Are you walking in your purpose toward your destiny, where you should be? Are you walking in the light or trying to trip me?

Are you headed to the church house—it's Sunday, you know? Are you headed to the place your big feet should not go?

Are you walking on folks or stepping over the little man? Are you kicking someone or helping them to stand?

I don't know what size you wear in a shoe. But are you swift to run to mischief, or are you going telling others about Christ like Matthew 28 told you to do?

# Ain't Y'all Hungry?

April 2, 2016

Ain't y'all hungry? I don't understand.

All this good stuff—how do you sit? Why don't you reach
in with your hand?

There is milk for the young and there is meat.

Come on to the table and just eat.

This is a free meal; the price is paid.

Been prepared, set, and laid.

Read the Word, or just listen to the preacher as he tell.

Freely eat and drink of the living water springing up like a
well.

This is good for your soul and daily walk.

Strength, courage, and how to treat others and talk.

You got an emptiness you just can't fill.

Partake of Jesus—He can and He will.

Ain't y'all hungry? I mean for this power to be in you?

O taste and see—that's what you need to do.

# No Nappy Head

2017

No nappy head, as I look throughout the congregation

I see no nappy head from any generation

The young, the old, women and men

I see styles held by spritz, gel, and hair pin

I see honey blonde, auburn, black, and gray

But I see no nappy head today

I see long, short, and bald; I see braided, sewed in, and glued in

Some curls, others finger waved, and others straighter than it's ever been

Put up the straightening comb, get the flat iron, put up the rollers, it can make curls too

I see no nappy head—we got all kinds of hairdo

Twist are in; wigs look real

Do it yourself. or go professional and pay the bill

I see no nappy head

You can get it fixed for a month or two; some you can wash and dry

The synthetic is cheap, but the human hair is high

But as I look throughout the congregation

I see no nappy head from any generation

# I Know Where the Men Are

October 1, 2017

They at the ball game—football, basketball, or baseball;
that's where they be

Some at the car wash; drive by there and see

Some of them at the dog show with the top breed—no mutt

Some at the barber shop, getting a haircut

Some at the lake, trying to catch fish

Others are in the restaurants, eating their favorite dish

Some at the rodeo, watching the cowboy ride

Some at the car show, showing off their fast, cool car with
tires twenty-four inches wide

Some at the gun show to see what they can buy; others at
the club or bar, just sitting day after day

Some running a marathon or the 5k

Some at the mall, looking good

But others at the laundromat in the hood

Some at the park, watching the children play

Some at the casino, gambling all his check away

Some like to play video or dominoes or go to the bingo hall

Some at the airport, hoping the plane don't fall

Some at the gym or fitness center, getting real stout

Others at the bachelor party or birthday party, blowing
candles out

Some at the bus station, sitting side by side

Some in the military, serving our country with pride

Some in a library, with a book in his face

Some in college, trying to get a degree

Some at the courthouse, hoping to be set free
Some at the company picnic, others in the plant or mill

Some at the doctor's office because of how they feel

Some at the grocery store; items on sale

Others at the post office, checking their mail

Some at your class reunion you have known for years

Some are at the funeral, but they probably in tears

Go to the festival or county fair

Go to the concert—you will find them there

Some at the auction, making a bid

Others may be at amusement park—this his weekend with his kid

Go to the street dance downtown

They be at the horse races at the Louisiana downs

Go to the farmers' market; they will be getting vegetables and fruit

They will be in church and have on a suit

But are they worthy?

# What You Working For?

July 4, 2004

People on the job work for pay.

Parents work so the children have a better way.

The eagle flies and the mail run.

We just got paid—now let's have some fun.

Don't forget the bills and things you need.

Overtime is okay, but don't get full of greed.

I know you want the weekend off, and holidays too.

When you retire, what will you do?

The pay is good and the benefits sure help cut a bunch.

You enjoy your job, so you work through lunch.

You educate your children and buy a home, car, motorcycle, boat, and Jet Ski.

You're living big, but don't forget to speak to me.

Every month the note is due.

What you working for? is what I am asking you.

When life comes to its end, what have you to show?

Will you leave good, lasting memories, or will you just go?

Have you lived a life pleasing and brought joy?

Did you teach a lesson on your journey to some girl or boy?

Did you help others and show the way?

Did you often have kind words to say?

Do you work for the Lord and serve Him every day?

Read, pray, worship, and witness.

Why are you even here anyway?

# Who You Talking To?

Who you talking to? Lower your voice, don't yell.

I heard you—it's a scam; what they sending in the mail?

You were on the phone over an hour.

You need to talk to the electric company; we have lost power.

They call awful late—it's after ten.

Who was that just left the mall, how much did they spend?

You can't believe everything—people busybody, tale-bearer and drama every day.

Do they got pull to get you on day shift?

They driving that nice car; will they give you lift?

Just who you talking to? Need to talk to Jesus.

# Poems Concerning Our Nation

# It's Independence Day!

September 30, 2015

We celebrate our nation being free; our flag pop in the wind
like the fireworks that so widespread, displaying in the
night air under the stars so bright.

The neighborhood comes out to eat barbecue, cooked on
the grill with care and right.

Go to the lake. Fish or swim. Play cards or dominoes and
watch the children play.

It's the 4th of July—it's Independence Day!

Let down the tailgate and sit around under the tree.

No drugs, no alcohol—just a big jar of lemon tea.

Let freedom ring! We left the mother country, not on our
own choice. But some got it good.

Real freedom comes when we accept Christ, as we should.

# Veteran

2017

You enlisted in the military, and you didn't have to.

You trained hard and stood tall, and I want to say thank you.

You knew your post and station.

Thank you for the freedom you gave to the next generation.

You had to leave your kin and fly far away.

You received medals and stripes, but thank you is all I can say.

Even if you were not a hero, we won the fight!

I hope there will be no more war—it just ain't right.

# Poems Concerning Life and Death

# Mother's Day Again

It's Mother's Day again, and the roses are blooming so red.

I wanted to get you something, but you went on ahead.

I would have got you a dress, or we could have went out to
eat and got fed.

But you went on ahead.

We could have rode around and sightsee wherever our
minds led, but…

I'll just think about what you taught me before you went on
ahead.

You showed us how to go by the way you led.

I will stay in Christ and in the church… you went on ahead.

# You Won't Be Home for Christmas

December 2014

You won't be home for Christmas this year.

We will miss you and shed many a tear.

It's not because you're on the road to make a delivery—
that's not why.

You won't be home for Christmas because you are away
beyond the sky.

We put up no tree nor light; just not feeling well.

Don't even want to shop; don't care what's on sale.

I try to lead the kids the best I can, and warn of sin.

The girl is a young lady and the boys are young men.

There is a space where you used to be.

If it were possible, tell Momma and Daddy howdy for me.

Every time I see an eighteen-wheeler, I read the name.

I know the driver couldn't be you—that's insane!

We often mention things you said.

You won't be home for Christmas; you're resting, not dead.

# Are Y'all Ready?

August 31, 2016

He found another land—a place he had not been

You too one day must travel to that place, but we just don't know when

Make sure you are ready and things are right; is your heart clean?

Are you ready to go to that land? It is the most beautiful place you have ever seen

Jesus is there; no need for the sun—He makes it shine

Don't worry about him; he will be fine

You just prepare yourself and make very certain of your soul today

Are you ready; do you know the way?

Go ahead, cry—that's no shame

Just be ready when He calls your name

You have the memories and keep them in your mind and heart

Live your life for the Lord; and if you have not, now is a good time to start

No more suffering, no more pain

Peace, rest, and heaven to gain

Family, be comforted in knowing one day these occasions will no more be

If there is anything I can do for the family and friends, please tell me

May the mighty arm of our God hold you tight

Comfort, strengthen, help, and keep you, all day and all night

Have no doubt and make certain you know

You will one day live for eternity; where will you go?

Thanks be to my Father God, and to my Savior Jesus, and to the sweet Holy Spirit for this gift and ability. Much appreciation to my pastor, Dr. Darnell Wagner, and to the Oak Grove Baptist Church of Wright City, Oklahoma, and to the Southeast District, and all friends.

CPSIA information can be obtained
at www.ICGtesting.com
Printed in the USA
BVHW041335230921
617401BV00014B/541

9 781637 696163